CW00864390

Bright Lights

&

Bold Hearts

STORIES FOR KIDS WHO DARE TO DREAM

FOREWORD BY UKAMAKA OLISAKWE

Bright Lights

&

Bold Hearts

STORIES FOR KIDS WHO DARE TO DREAM

BY OKENNA NZELU

Bright Lights Books

BRIGHT LIGHTS BOOKS

We are a publishing company focused on bringing stories about Africa to young readers across the world.

We work with authors and artists across Africa to publish stories of fiction, short biographies, essays and poems which are inspiring a generation of young readers.

If you are a writer or an artist with a story to tell, we would love to hear from you.

www.brightlightsbooks.com

contact@brightlightsbooks.com

First published in Great Britain by Bright Lights Books 2021

This is a creative work of nonfiction

Editorial Direction and Art Direction by Okenna Nzelu

Inside Cover Art by Kofo Nolla Omidiran IG: @oknollao

Illustrations by Nimble Pencils

Printed in the UK by Biddles Books Limited

A CIP catalogue record for this book is available from the British Library

ISBN: 978-1-5272-7466-2

To our little lights

Foreword

Representation matters. I grew up in a small neighborhood in Kano in northern Nigeria. As a child, I had a collection of picture books that told stories of great achievers, mostly British and American people with blonde hair and blue or gray eyes, who were successful in science and sports and the arts. And although these books were inspirational, I did not belong in them. I felt like such successes happened to people who do not look like me. It did not also help that the religious literatures I was exposed to (My Book of Bible Stories, for example) were equally filled with blue-eyed people, and that the only black entity in those stories was the Devil.

This was despite the fact that I was surrounded by Nigerians who excelled in football, in mathematics, in music and movies, but since I was young and my access to certain media was restricted, I was left with the images in my picture books — of successful Europeans, of the Devil whose skin looked like mine, of limitations. These images became the only truth; I couldn't see myself outside of those constructs. Because there were no other images countering those hurtful constructs, I began to believe them. And for many years afterwards, I watched the people around me aspire to whiteness; they bleached their skin and straightened their hair, and while I strongly believe that people should do whatever they want with their bodies, my young mind at that time could not dissociate blackness from inferiority. It would take many years, after reading the works of African authors, before I began to disabuse myself of those harmful ideas and write books populated by people who look like me.

Okenna Nzelu understands how impressionable young children can be, and he has taken important steps in Bright Lights to change the narrative, to fill our children's libraries with images of people like themselves who are successful, who are beautiful, who can be anything they want to be. At 15, I wanted to be a musician and could sing along to everything by Mariah Carey and Celine Dion. I wrote songs about love and relationships which my poor siblings were obligated to listen to, and felt that songs by the likes of Nelly Uchendu and Onyeka Onwenu and Christy Essien-Igbokwe were too local, too ordinary.

Perhaps I would not have attempted lightening my skin with dangerous creams at the age of 18, had my library been filled with stories of people like Angélique Kidjo, who started performing at the age of 6 and grew up on the sounds of Miriam Makeba, Manu Dibango, and Hugh Masekela. I would not have approached science in senior secondary school with a defeatist attitude, had I read about people like Sossina M. Haile, whose family escaped political persecution, excelled in her educational pursuits, and went on to become a world leading scientist.

Okenna understands what is at stake. He knows that images were used to infiltrate the minds of young African children and pollute them, and he knows that images must be used to mend and empower them.

One of the beauties of Bright Lights is how far-reaching it is. In it, we read about great achievers from different communities across the African continent, who refuse to succumb in the face of adversity — be it economic, religious, or political — and went on to succeed in their endeavours. Their stories are relatable; these are the people we know, from communities we grew up in, and conditions we endured. Even when Okenna describes the struggles of the people in the book, he does so with optimism. And through it all, with every bright stroke and appropriately toned shade of skin, any young child reading this book will feel included, seen.

— Ukamaka Olisakwe

January 2021

Vermillion, S.D.

Contents

Introduction

Artists & Authors

Athletes

Entrepreneurs

INNOVATORS & SCIENTISTS

LEADERS & HUMANITARIANS

EXTRAS

Introduction

When I decided to write this book, I had what I thought was a very simple goal of telling stories of everyday people who can inspire the next generation of young Africans.

Then I listened to a podcast while researching this book in which the speaker discusses "The Necessity of Aim". He explains, "In order to act in any sort of coherent manner, you must orient yourself towards a destination." So why do you need to aim for anything? What should you aim at achieving? What happens if you don't orient yourself towards anything? What happens if you do?

This book will provide many ideas and illustrate what happens when people, and specifically Africans, aim for something worthwhile and pursue it passionately.

One of the first questions I faced was how to select people for the book. I wanted to produce a book that was more focused on social impact rather than individual excellence. So while every person featured is inspirational and has achieved tremendous success in their careers, my hope is to show that they each pursue and work for a greater purpose.

My aspirations for this book have grown since I began writing it. This book will not only inspire and provide aim, but also spark a renewed interest in our young ones to develop an early habit of reading. Of course, this can't be done without the encouragement of parents and caregivers. Children who are encouraged to make a habit of reading will ultimately have a better chance of success in the world.

There is something empowering about seeing yourself reflected in the characters profiled in this book. I expect that certain people will resonate more strongly with you than others

A shortcoming of this book is that I have unwittingly tried to tell a whole life story in only a few words.

For any of these people or types of careers you're more interested in, I encourage you to investigate beyond the mini biographies of this book. There are lots of amazing stories and resources online.

Researching and writing this book has been a real joy for me and everyone who has helped bring it to life. Each story proves the impact every child born in Africa can have on society, irrespective of economic background, gender, religion or nationality. I hope this book impresses upon you the belief that the greatest fulfilment is to live a life full of purpose and consideration for society.

Artists & Authors

Angelique Kidjo

Singer, Activist
Cotonou, Benin

Angelique is one of the most popular music icons in the world and has won several Grammy Awards.

Angelique had always enjoyed singing. But in her country of Benin, children are often discouraged from focusing their careers on music and arts. It was no different for Angelique when she started singing at school.

"...My grandmother sat me down and cleaned and braided my hair, and I told her I didn't want to sing any more. She said: 'Are you going to let stupid people tell you what to do with your life? Do what you have to do.' To this day that advice is what has kept me going, and what has guided me." - Angelique Kidjo.

She started singing in her school band and continued until she had to leave Benin after she was banned by the government. She moved to France and worked as a cleaner and then as a hairdresser to make ends meet.

With the money she earned from her jobs, she paid for music lessons and continued to practice her music as a backup singer.

After a few years, Angelique had become one of the most popular live musicians in Paris and went on to record albums. Her talent and hard work have won her several Grammy Awards and made her a household name around the world.

Angelique has taken her purpose further than music. Through her Batonga Foundation, she works to give young girls and women in Africa the skills and knowledge to achieve great things. Her father and grandmother always encouraged her to pursue her dreams and she believes every young girl should do the same.

"YOUR BRAIN IS YOUR GREATEST WEAPON. CONNECT IT TO YOUR HEART, AND YOU CAN GO ANYWHERE."

Anglique Kidjo

★ Chimamanda Ngozi Adichie ★

Author
Enugu. Nigeria

Chimamanda's novels have inspired conversations around race, culture, gender and human dignity. She is an award-winning author and one of the world's leading novelists.

Chimamanda was born in the city of Enugu in Nigeria. She performed well at school and was offered a place to study medicine at the University of Nigeria, Nsukka. She had started studying medicine due to pressure from her family, however she knew her passion was in writing. So after a year, she left medical school and relocated to the USA where she completed her bachelor's degree and then earned a Master of Arts in Creative Writing.

While she was still at school, Chimamanda had begun writing short stories and plays. She also started writing her first novel while at university. The novel, Purple Hibiscus, was published in 2003 and marked her arrival as a talented storyteller. Chimamanda has gone on to publish four best-selling novels which have won her prestigious global awards.

Chinua Achebe spoke highly of her after reading her second novel, Half of a Yellow Sun: "We do not usually associate wisdom with beginners, but here is a new writer endowed with the gift of ancient storytellers. Adichie knows what is at stake, and what to do about it."

Chimamanda has been vocal about fairness and equality in the way men and women are treated. Through her work, she encourages young girls to understand that they deserve the same opportunities and privileges which are given to boys.

Every year, Chimamanda hosts a free workshop in Nigeria offering coaching and advice to young writers. Her annual workshop has been running for more than ten years and has over 200 alumni, including Eloghosa Osunde and Ayobami Adebayo.

"I THINK YOU TRAVEL TO SEARCH AND YOU COME BACK HOME TO FIND YOURSELF THERE."

Chimamanda Ngozi Adichie

Genevieve Nnaji

Actress, Director, Producer
Imo, Nigeria

Genevieve Nnaji has helped make the Nigerian film industry (Nollywood) what it is today.

Genevieve's first role as an actress was when she was eight years old where she featured in the popular soap opera "Ripples". She always knew she wanted to be an actress and this focus has helped her succeed in the movie industry. Genevieve grew up in Lagos and studied creative arts at the University of Lagos.

While she was at university, she started auditioning for roles in Nollywood films. After numerous rejections, she was eventually offered a role in a film called "Most Wanted" at the age of 19. This was the real beginning of her Nollywood career. She has now starred in more than 200 films.

Genevieve continued to learn and study her craft over the years. She has even started producing and directing her own films while also acting in them.

In 2018, she directed the film "Lionheart", which became the first Nigerian film to be submitted to the Oscars. "Lionheart" was bought by Netflix in the same year, making it the first Netflix Original film from Nigeria.

Genevieve believes every girl has the right to do whatever she wants to do, and to go as far as her ambition takes her. She spends her time outside work promoting equal rights for girls and supports charities that help girls who have survived abuse.

Her contributions to Nollywood earned her the MFR honour by the Nigerian President in 2011.

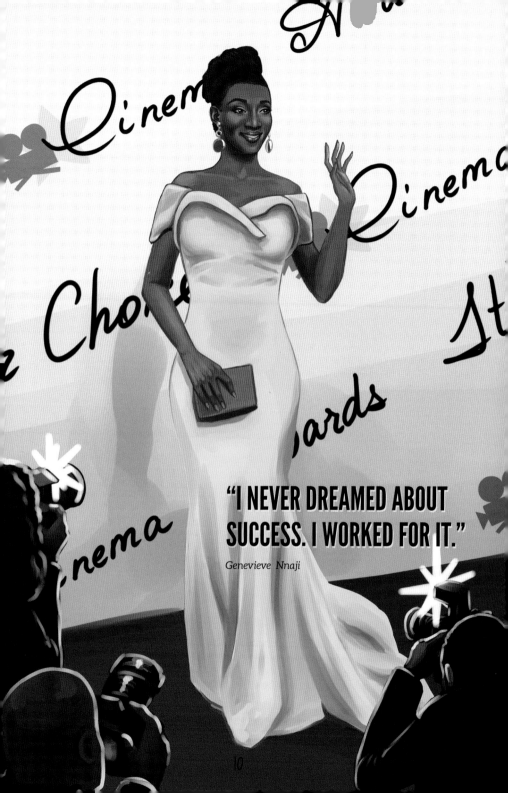

"I NEVER DREAMED ABOUT SUCCESS. I WORKED FOR IT."

Genevieve Nnaji

Ibrahim Mahama

Artist, Author
Bole, Ghana

Ibrahim is a world-renowned artist and is respected as one of the most promising talents of his generation.

Ibrahim was born in Ghana where he grew up. His parents sent him to boarding school in Ghana for secondary school. He believes this experience helped him to grow creatively. Afterwards, Ibrahim studied art at Kwame Nkrumah University of Science and Technology and received his Master of Fine Arts from the same university.

While still at university, Ibrahim attended an art exhibition called "Documenta 13", which helped him understand his purpose and ambitions as an artist.

Ibrahim's talent was soon noticed by a group of international art curators while he was finishing his degree. Since then, he has developed his work further and featured in art exhibitions around the world. He has achieved all this while remaining in Ghana, where he hopes to pave the way for the next generation of African artists.

His art carries a message of hope and promise, which he expresses through different mediums. He is best known for transforming old materials, such as sacks, and using them to create beautiful works of art.

In 2019, Ibrahim opened the Savannah Centre for Contemporary Art in Tamale as his contribution to art in Ghana. The centre provides artists with working space, residency and a world class research hub.

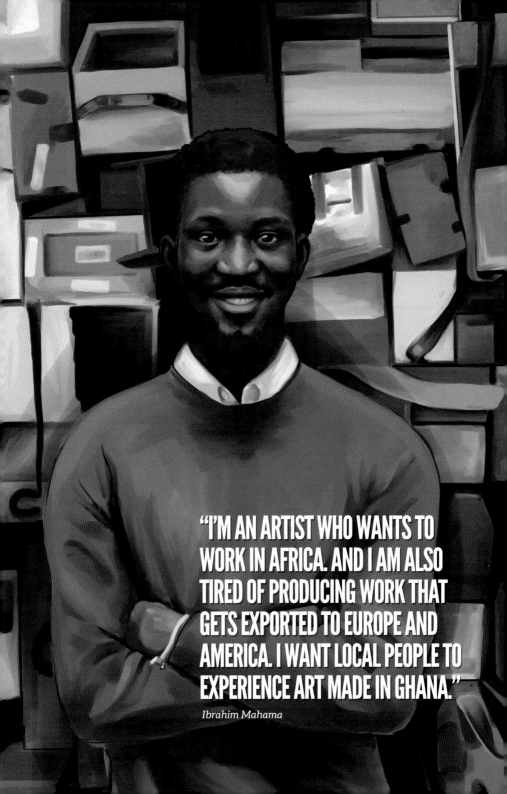

"I'M AN ARTIST WHO WANTS TO WORK IN AFRICA. AND I AM ALSO TIRED OF PRODUCING WORK THAT GETS EXPORTED TO EUROPE AND AMERICA. I WANT LOCAL PEOPLE TO EXPERIENCE ART MADE IN GHANA."

Ibrahim Mahama

Laduma Ngxokolo

Designer, Fashion, Entrepreneur
Port Elizabeth, South Africa

Laduma created an international fashion brand that is recognised all over the world for its high quality.

Born and raised in South Africa, Laduma took an interest in fabrics as a child after his mother came home with a knitting machine. He later used this knitting machine to make scarves, which he sold to pay for food and his bus fare to school.

He continued learning about textiles at school and went on to study textile design at Nelson Mandela University. He loved his studies so much that he read every day and practiced making lots of different patterns. In his final year at university, he received a bursary in South Africa and began to consider setting up his own factory.

After his studies, Laduma started his clothing company with the support of Nelson Mandela University. He made a number of mistakes and lost most of his money shortly after he started.

However, he kept learning and improving his designs until he received an order for 200 pieces, which gave him enough money to grow his business further.

His company has continued to grow and in 2018 his dream came true – he bought a manufacturing factory in South Africa. Through his factory and brand, Maxhosa, he employs more than 100 people and is able to manufacture his own products in Africa. He has received several awards for his work in fashion, including the Vogue Italia Sousing for Africa Award.

Laduma knows that goods produced in Africa can be of the same or even better quality as goods produced anywhere else in the world. This is his mission with Maxhosa.

"AS A BRAND, I WANT TO RECLAIM THE DIGNITY AND CONFIDENCE OF AFRICAN CULTURE."

Laduma Ngxokolo

Maaza Mengiste

Author
Addis Ababa, Ethiopia

Maaza's books have reshaped the way in which world history is told. Her second book, The Shadow King, was shortlisted for the prestigious Booker Prize in 2020.

Maaza was born in Addis Ababa and lived there until the Ethiopian revolution of 1974 when it became unsafe for her family. Her family left Ethiopia and spent the next few years living in Nigeria and then Kenya. They eventually settled in the USA where she continued her education.

After Maaza graduated from university, she got a job working as a business consultant. It was the ideal job for a young university graduate, but Maaza knew it wasn't right for her. She would spend her evenings working at a bar just to relax and unwind from her day job.

She continued searching for her passion until she was offered her dream job as a screenplay writer. But it turned out this job didn't give her the opportunity to create authentic stories either.

At this point, even though she had never even written a short story, Maaza decided to take a risk and become a full-time writer. She then attended New York University for a master's degree in Creative Writing.

Maaza began spending all her weekends and evenings writing. Both her books have focused on key points in world history and the role Ethiopian women played in them. Alongside writing The Shadow King, Maaza founded Project 3541, which is a collection of photographs taken during Italy's 1935-41 invasion of Ethiopia. She is also involved in human rights work.

She advises young writers to develop a daily habit of reading and writing, even when they don't feel up to it.

"HOPE CAN NEVER COME
FROM DOING NOTHING."

Maaza Mengiste, Beneath the Lion's Gaze

★ Njideka Akunyili Crosby ★

Visual Artist
Enugu, Nigeria

Njideka is a world-renowned artist and was named one of TIME's 100 most influential people in the world.

As a young girl growing up in Enugu, Nigeria, Njideka thought she would someday become a doctor like her father. While playing with her friends at school, she would often pretend to be a hospital doctor treating a sick patient.

But when she turned 16, she took an art class and impressed her teacher, who encouraged her to continue taking art lessons. Njideka found that she enjoyed art lessons, so she continued to develop her talent.

After Njideka finished school, she moved to the USA and spent a lot of time studying art at universities, including at Yale and the Pennsylvania Academy of Fine Arts. Njideka's talent and hard work got her selected to become the Artist in Residence in 2011 at The Studio Museum in New York.

When Njideka got to New York, she met Wangechi Mutu who be-

came her mentor. As an already established artist, Wangechi generously offered advice and guidance to Njideka which helped to launch her career and she has now grown to be one of the most promising artists in the world. Through her paintings, she tells the story of her African culture in ways that everyone can relate to.

Njideka has since received a number of special awards for her work and takes part in exhibitions around the world. In 2016 she won the Financial Times Women of the Year award and in 2019 TIME magazine named her one of the next 100 most influential people in the world. Njideka still fondly remembers her childhood aspiration to become a doctor but is very happy to have followed her true passion and talent as an artist.

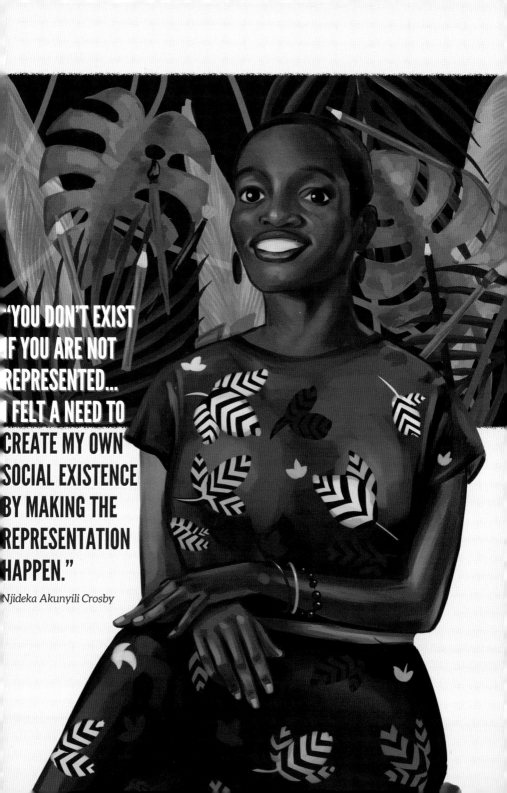

"YOU DON'T EXIST IF YOU ARE NOT REPRESENTED... I FELT A NEED TO CREATE MY OWN SOCIAL EXISTENCE BY MAKING THE REPRESENTATION HAPPEN."

Njideka Akunyili Crosby

Athletes

★ Anthony Oluwafemi Joshua ★

World Heavyweight Boxing Champion
Watford, UK

Antony is a two-time world heavyweight boxing champion and Olympic gold medalist.

His parents were born in Nigeria but moved to England to pursue a better life for their family. Anthony was born a few years later in Watford.

Anthony enjoyed running and playing football at school, but he also got into a lot of trouble as a teenager growing up in London. After being charged with a criminal offense and spending two weeks in prison, Anthony decided to turn his life around. At 18, he moved away from his friends and began training to become a world class boxer.

For Anthony, discipline meant running every morning, spending more than ten hours at the gym every day, eating nutritious food and training his mind by playing chess. Through hard work and determination, Anthony pushed beyond his limits to win his first major championship only three years after taking up boxing.

In the following years, Anthony won the gold medal at the London Olympics and became a unified heavyweight champion.

Anthony was awarded an OBE for his services to sports by Prince Charles in 2018. In December 2019, he fought and defeated Andy Ruiz to become a two-time heavyweight boxing champion.

Anthony has visited the Makoko slums in Lagos several times where he reminds children that they can break through all limitations. He also supports the work of charities focused on turning around the lives of young offenders and those at risk of going to prison. Anthony recalls the challenges he faced as a teenager growing up in North London and this motivates him in his work to help teenagers to fulfil their ambitions.

"AS LONG AS YOU HAVE DISCIPLINE, YOU CAN BE A SUCCESS. DISCIPLINE IS WHAT MAKES YOU DO EVERYTHING YOU NEED TO DO."

Anthony Oluwafemi Joshua

Caster Semenya

Athlete, Footballer
Limpopo Province, South Africa

Caster is an Olympic gold medallist and one of the fastest women in the world.

Caster was born in a small village in South Africa, near the border with Botswana. Growing up, she was interested in sports and preferred playing with the boys even though she had three sisters. At school, she played football and only began running as a way to train for football.

As she got older, she focused more on her running and she began to win most of her races. Caster continued to train and practice daily until she was ready to compete in global championships. She won the World Championships in Berlin when she was 18 and, later that year, Track and Field News voted her the number one women's 800m runner of the year.

At the World Championships, she was so fast that the organisers became suspicious and decided to investigate her for performance-enhancing drug use.

When Caster won the 2016 Olympic gold medal, she became the fastest 800m female runner in the world. She had previously won a gold medal in the 2012 Olympics, and won a total of 31 races in a row until she was ruled out of competing.

After a series of tests, it was concluded that Caster was born with naturally high levels of testosterone. Caster was born with traits that allow her to be an exceptional athlete, and she has trained to develop that talent. However, the ruling against her remains in place.

Since the World Athletics ruling, Caster has gone on to become a football star playing for JVW FC in South Africa. She holds a university degree in sports science and has also partnered with a charity to improve girls' health in Africa.

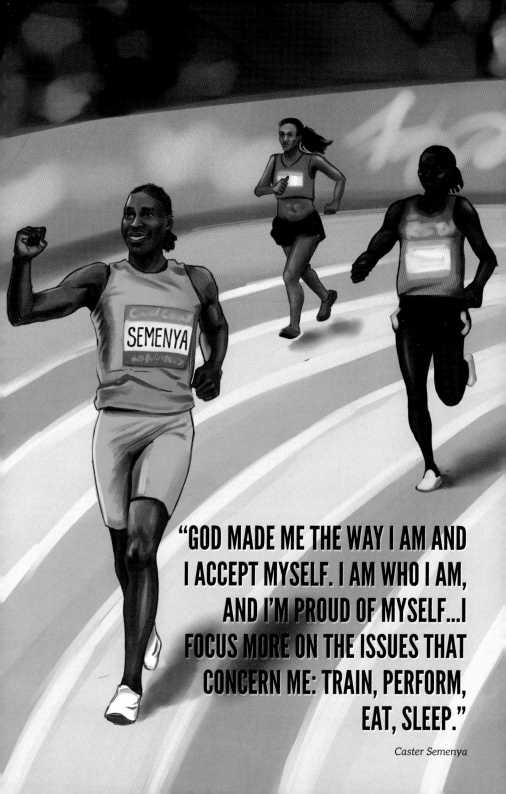

"GOD MADE ME THE WAY I AM AND I ACCEPT MYSELF. I AM WHO I AM, AND I'M PROUD OF MYSELF...I FOCUS MORE ON THE ISSUES THAT CONCERN ME: TRAIN, PERFORM, EAT, SLEEP."

Caster Semenya

Didier Drogba

Footballer, Peace Ambassador
Abidjan, Côte d'Ivoire

Didier is an all-time top scorer and former captain of the Ivory Coast national team, and the first African player to score 100 goals in the Premier League.

Didier was born in Abidjan, where he spent most of his childhood. After school, he often played football at a car park with his friends. But after both his parents lost their jobs in Ivory Coast, he relocated to France to live with his uncle.

By the time Didier was 13, he was playing football every day and had stopped focusing on his schoolwork. His grades fell, and he went from being at the top of his class to repeating a year. Didier's parents decided to ban him from playing football until his grades improved. He remains grateful that his parents did that because even as a successful footballer he understands how important a good education is.

Didier was not an immediate success in football but he continued to practice and did not give up.

In his first few years, he was frequently injured and missed quite a few matches. By the age of 21, he had never attended a football academy or had any formal football training. Eventually, he was noticed by several big clubs and signed by Chelsea.

Outside of football, Didier has played a vital role bringing peace to his country. After leading his country to qualify for the 2006 World Cup finals, Didier picked up a microphone live on national television and begged both warring factions to lay down their arms and stop the fighting. Within a week, the Ivorian government and opposing forces began talks which led to the end of the Ivorian war. Didier now spends his time on his charity, and has donated money to build a hospital in his hometown.

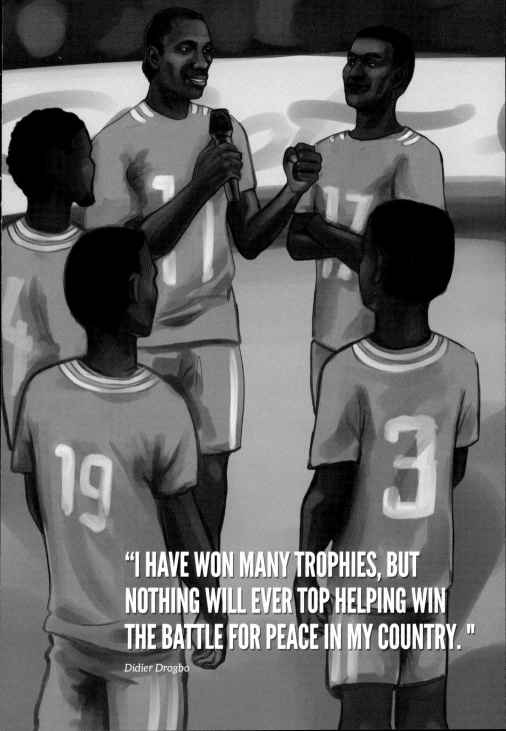

"I HAVE WON MANY TROPHIES, BUT NOTHING WILL EVER TOP HELPING WIN THE BATTLE FOR PEACE IN MY COUNTRY."

Didier Drogbo

Dikembe Mutombo

Basketball Player, Humanitarian
Kinshasa, Democratic Republic of Congo

Dikembe was an NBA All-Star who is now focused on improving living conditions in Democratic Republic of the Congo.

Dikembe was the seventh of ten children, born in Kinshasa. His father, who was a teacher, taught them to value education but also to look after the less fortunate. As a boy, Dikembe hoped to become a doctor. He was awarded a scholarship to study medicine at Georgetown University in the USA.

He did not grow up playing basketball. In fact, he was already 17 when his brother took him to a basketball court for the first time. While studying medicine at Georgetown, Dikembe continued to practice and improve his basketball skills. He had to learn the game very quickly to catch up with his peers. Eventually, he was noticed by the team coach and asked to join the university basketball team. He graduated from Georgetown University with a bachelor's degree in Linguistics and Diplomacy after switching from medicine.

Dikembe's persistence paid off after university when he was drafted into the NBA to play for the Denver Nuggets, and Dikembe became one of the greatest defensive basketball players ever. He made his mark as a feared defender with his power and height. Dikembe was among the top three defensive players in the NBA for nine consecutive years. Over his career, he averaged more than ten rebounds per game.

He is an eight-time NBA All-Star and four-time NBA Defensive Player of the Year. He retired after 18 seasons in the NBA and was inducted into the Basketball Hall of Fame.

Dikembe has dedicated his life to improving living conditions for people in his country. He built and opened the Biamba Marie Mutombo hospital near Kinshasa, which has now served over 140,000 people.

Siya Kolisi

Rugby Player, Leader
Port Elizabeth, South Africa

Siya was the first African captain for the South African rugby team and is one of the greatest sports leaders in the world.

Siya's childhood in South Africa was very difficult. His mother gave birth to him when she was just 17 and he grew up with no money and very little food at home. Siya began to play rugby before he was ten years old and by 12 he was offered a scholarship that paid for his education.

Siya had the physical size and speed to be a talented rugby player but he quickly learnt the importance of hard work when he joined his high school rugby team. "I was running on talent for a while and those who worked harder than me were catching up and getting past me. No matter how talented you are, you still have to work hard."

As Siya improved his work ethic, his performance also improved and he was spotted by rugby scouts who invited him to the national under-18 rugby union team. He later earned his place in the South Africa under-20

side before being invited to join the national team in 2013. In 2018, Siya was appointed captain of the South African rugby team. One year later, he led his team to win the rugby world cup in Japan.

South Africa has a complicated history which is partly to blame for it being financially unequal. The majority indigenous African population have very little wealth and continue to suffer economic hardships according to the South African Human Rights Commission.

Siya is very passionate about doing all he can to give children in South Africa the opportunity to be successful. He has gone to one of the poorest communities to build a new rugby field for children. Outside of rugby, he hopes to inspire other people to achieve their dreams irrespective of race.

"WHEN I WALK OUT ON THE FIELD I WANT TO BE THE BEST FLANKER IN THE WORLD. IF YOU THINK IN RACIAL TERMS, YOU ARE LIMITING YOURSELF AND YOUR HORIZONS."

Siya Kolisi

Entrepreneurs

Aliko Dangote

Entrepreneur, Industrialist, Philanthropist
Kano, Nigeria

Aliko has created industries and thousands of jobs across Africa. He is also one of the most charitable people in the world.

Aliko was born in Kano State, Nigeria. As a primary school student, he bought cartons of sweets which he sold to his classmates to make money. Aliko had always been interested in business. After graduating from university in Egypt, he got a loan from his uncle and started trading sugar, cement, rice and fish in Nigeria. He was so successful, he managed to pay back his uncle's loan after only a year.

He later started his own company and called it the Dangote Group. Aliko soon moved into manufacturing to ensure that goods were produced in Africa at an even better quality, and his company has now expanded to include exports.

Before Dangote's expansion, African countries depended on foreign manufacturers to supply them with goods such as cement, sugar and salt.

As an example, every year Nigeria spent a lot of money importing cement from Europe until Aliko built cement plants to meet the country's needs.

A similar situation exists with petroleum, which Nigeria spends billions of dollars importing every year. Aliko's oil refinery will ensure that West Africa produces its own petroleum while creating jobs and opportunities for thousands of people.

By creating jobs locally, he also helps ensure more money for state governments through taxes. Aliko says "for too long, we have been exporting jobs and importing poverty."

Aliko's foundation is the largest private charity in Africa and focuses on improving lives of children through healthcare and education.

Bayo Ogunlesi

Investor, Entrepreneur
Ogun, Nigeria

Bayo has owned some of the largest airports in the world and now advises African countries on improving standards of living.

As a young boy, Bayo went to school at Kings College, Lagos. Bayo had always been highly ambitious and did very well at school. However, he didn't like maths and knew he would have to spend a lot of time practicing to get better. He worked so hard ahead of his final exams at Kings College that his results got him admitted into the University of Oxford.

He later became a lawyer after graduating from Harvard Law School. When he decided to become a banker, he didn't know much about banking but was always willing to learn. He spent several years working in banks, and had become the head of an investment bank by the time he left to start his own company. Bayo had been fully focused on his career and living a quiet life until he dared to buy one of the world's busiest airports, Gatwick airport in London. The landmark deal threw his name into the spotlight.

His advice on succeeding was that "success is about ability, hard work and relationships". Through the relationships he built while working as an investment banker, Bayo was able to raise enough money to buy Gatwick Airport. He made a lot of improvements to the airport and later sold it for a substantial profit. Bayo knows he would not have been able to buy the airport without his relationships, and that's why he considers maintaining good relationships to be one of the most important ingredients for success.

Bayo now spends a lot of his time advising African countries on how to make life better for their people through his work as a Non-Executive Chairman of the Africa Finance Corporation.

"MAY YOUR DREAMS BE YOUR ONLY BOUNDARIES."

Bayo Ogunesi

★ Bethlehem Tilahun Alemu ★

Social Entrepreneur
Addis Ababa, Ethiopia

Bethlehem has created thousands of jobs and has been listed within the 100 Most Powerful Women in the World

Ethiopia is one of the most beautiful countries in the world. It may also be the oldest country in the world. However, Bethlehem grew up in Ethiopia during a difficult time for the country. There were not many jobs for the grown-ups and lots of children were not able to go to school.

When Bethlehem was 24, she decided to do something to create jobs for people in her community: she began making shoes in her grandmother's workshop and selling them. As she sold more and more shoes, her business grew and she was able to pay more and more people to work for her.

Bethlehem now sells 125,000 shoes every year in countries around the world. Also, she has created more than a thousand well-paid jobs for people who help her produce and sell the shoes.

Because of her success, Bethlehem has continued to expand into other business areas. She sells leather products and also produces some of the best coffee in the world. The materials for everything she makes is sourced from Ethiopia because she believes in the talent and resources of her country.

She often says that running a business is not easy, but if you are determined to succeed, it is a very good way to change people's lives for the better.

"FOR PEOPLE TO BE INNOVATIVE... THEY DON'T HAVE TO REALLY TRAVEL A LONG WAY OR COPY SOMEBODY'S BUSINESS IDEA. IT'S RIGHT HERE."

Bethlehem Tilahun Alemu

Mo Ibrahim

Business Leader, Entrepreneur, Philanthropist
Eshket, Sudan

Mo is often described as the boy from Sudan who brought mobile phones to Africa.

Mo was born in Sudan but his family moved to Egypt when he was a young boy. He was very curious as a child, always trying to learn and understand how things worked. He enjoyed reading about the newest technology and eventually went on to study engineering at university in Egypt.

When he graduated, he got his dream job at British Telecom. After Mo had worked at British Telecom for a few years, things were not going as well as he had expected. He eventually resigned and decided to start his own telecoms company using everything he had learnt as well as relying on the people he had met. He had very little money, but he didn't let that deter him.

Mo founded Celtel in 1998, and seven years later more than 100 million people in Africa had mobile phones.

Mo has said he would never have been successful if he didn't surround himself with very smart people. He understands his knowledge is limited and so depends on advice from more knowledgeable people around him.

"Any money I'm going to make here in Africa...I'm going to put it back into Africa." - Mo Ibrahim

After a few years, he decided to sell his company. But Mo is still busy working to make Africa a better place. He launched the Mo Ibrahim Prize for African Leadership to celebrate African leaders who have helped develop their countries and strengthen democracy for the benefit of their people.

"IT IS AN HONOUR TO HAVE BEEN SELECTED FOR THE MO IBRAHIM PRIZE... IT IS MY HOPE THAT WOMEN AND GIRLS ACROSS AFRICA WILL BE INSPIRED TO REACH THEIR TRUE POTENTIAL ...AND TO PURSUE THEIR DREAMS."

Ellen Johnson Sirleaf

Patrice Motsepe

Entrepreneur, Lawyer, Philanthropist
Soweto, South Africa

Patrice is the founder of African Rainbow Minerals, the most successful mining company in Africa.

Patrice was born in Soweto, the son of a teacher who owned a Spaza shop. Patrice began working in his father's shop from the age of five. His father would wake him up at 5am every morning and he would sometimes work at the shop until midnight. While he worked long and hard, this experience taught him a lot about business.

He later went to University of Witwatersrand where he graduated with a law degree. Upon graduation, he was offered a job at a law firm in South Africa where he rose to become a partner. After many years working as a lawyer, Patrice founded his own company to offer mining services.

A few years later, he began buying gold and platinum mines that no one else wanted. He was able to make a profit from these mines by giving his workers shares in the company,

which motivated them to cut costs and increase productivity. Patrice was then able to expand his business further and buy more mines in South Africa. He has spent the past 25 years building his company to become the most successful mining company in Africa.

Patrice believes everyone is at their best when allowed to pursue careers in the area they are most passionate about. In 2013, Patrice pledged to give away half of everything he owns to poor and disadvantaged Africans. He began the Motsepe Foundation to support communities and small businesses in South Africa. Through donations, Patrice has helped to establish and support more than 1,500 youth-owned businesses in South Africa.

YOUTH
FORUM
AFRICA

"PREPARING FOR THE FUTURE BEGINS WITH GETTING A GOOD EDUCATION. THAT'S THE MOST IMPORTANT THING YOU CAN DO, AND STUDY IN THE AREA THAT YOU LOVE. BECOME THAT WHICH EXCITES YOU THE MOST."

Patrice Motsepe

Strive Masiyiwa

Innovator, Philanthropist
Southern Zimbabe, Zimbabwe

Strive has used his wealth to provide scholarships to more than 250,000 African children and orphans.

Strive was born in Zimbabwe at a time when there was very little freedom for native Zimbabweans. The Europeans living in Zimbabwe had land ownership privileges and Strive's family was forced to flee Zimbabwe. He ended up completing his education in Britain, where he studied electrical engineering at university. After his studies, Strive came back home to Zimbabwe to help bring positive change to his country.

Strive decided to start his own company in Zimbabwe using the little money he had saved from working as an engineer. His company initially sold electrical products. As mobile phones became more popular around the world, he expanded his business to mobile phone technology. He sold the service to millions of people in Zimbabwe, helping to improve communication.

Strive's company is one of the largest companies in Zimbabwe and now operates in more than 20 countries around the world. He has created jobs for thousands of Africans and he continues to look for ways to influence people's lives positively.

Today, Strive is generally recognised as one of the most generous people in the world. He continues to use his knowledge and influence to help develop Africa, while he uses his wealth to provide education for children in Africa who are unable to afford it.

"A VISION ON ITS OWN IS NOT ENOUGH.
HARD WORK AND DEDICATION IS REQUIRED
TO MAKE THAT VISION A REALITY."

Strive Masiyiwa

Tewolde Gebremariam

Airline CEO, Executive
Addis Ababa, Ethiopia

Tewolde is the Chief Executive of Africa's largest airline, Ethiopian Airlines, based in Addis Ababa.

Tewolde was born in Ethiopia and studied Economics at Addis Ababa University. He applied and got a job at Ethiopian Airlines after graduating from university. As a child, Tewolde had loved planes so he was excited to learn everything about the business of aviation. Tewolde began working as a junior in the cargo department before later moving to sales.

When the managers at Ethiopian Airlines needed someone to take on a new or important job, they would always call Tewolde because of his dedication and work ethic. As a result, he was promoted and given more opportunities to grow within the company. After a few more years working in sales and helping the airline grow, he rose to senior positions and was later appointed as the Chief Executive Officer.

Ethiopian Airlines owns a fleet of more than 125 planes and flies to more than 120 cities around the world. Tewolde has also helped establish other airlines in West and South Africa.

Tewolde's job as the CEO of Ethiopian Airlines is sometimes very challenging. In 2019, there was an accident that changed the lives of 157 families. During this difficult time, Tewolde stopped all flights and vowed that the tragedy would not define Ethiopian Airlines. He has continued to rebuild confidence in the airline since then and works to make air travel even safer for everyone.

Tewolde was named Best African Business Leader and African CEO of the Year in 2012.

"IN LIFE, WHERE YOU START MAY NOT MATTER.
WHAT MATTERS MOST IS HOW YOU MAKE USE OF
EVERY OPPORTUNITY YOU GET."

Tewolde Gebremariam

Tidjane Thiam

Business Executive
Abidjan, Côte d'Ivoire

Tidjane was the first African to lead a major European bank.

Tidjane was born in Côte d'Ivoire after the country's independence. His father had moved there from Senegal. Both his parents were from prominent families in West Africa, so they were able to provide Tidjane with a good quality education. Tidjane's success at school resulted in him becoming the first Ivorian to pass the entrance examination into École Polytechnique in Paris. He then graduated at the top of his class and was offered a scholarship to study for his MBA at INSEAD.

Tidjane began his career working as a management consultant, advising companies on how to achieve long-term growth. He later joined the Ivorian government to contribute to his country's development. However, after the Ivorian coup in 1999, he was arrested and detained for several weeks. After that experience, he decided that politics was not for him and went back to the world of business.

He returned to Europe and became a very successful management consultant. In 2015 Tidjane was appointed the CEO of Credit Suisse, which employs more than 45,000 people around the world. His performance in turning the bank around and growing the bank's profits proved that he was the best person for the job. Tidjane never forgot how important it is to stay connected to his home – he remains a member of the Africa Progress Panel, a group with the purpose of effecting positive change in Africa.

"How do I feel about my life? I get up in the morning, and I try to do my best. And I do that every day, one day at a time."

"WHAT MAKES THE DIFFERENCE IS NOT HOW HIGH YOU CAN GO BUT HOW LOW YOU CAN GO. RAISE YOUR MINIMUM, BECAUSE THAT WILL DEFINE YOUR POTENTIAL IN LIFE."

Tidjane Thiam

Innovators & Scientists

★ Diébédo Francis Kéré ★

Architect, Professor
Gando, Burkina Faso

Francis is a world-renowned architect whose buildings and designs have been recognised internationally with awards including the Global Holcim Award Gold.

Francis was born and grew up in a village called Gando in Burkina Faso. He was the first child from his village to attend school. When Francis turned seven, he had to leave his family to live in the city with his uncle as there were no schools in Gando. When he finished school, he decided to become a carpenter and began working with wood in Burkina Faso.

At 18, having done well at school and also learnt carpentry, he won a scholarship to study woodworking in Germany. Once there, he decided to study architecture instead because he believed it would be more useful to his country. During his final year at university, he designed a primary school for his hometown in Gando and then raised the money to build it.

He later started his own company called Kéré Architecture, which employs a team of architects and architecture students. His company has designed buildings in several countries around the world including the United States, China, Kenya, Uganda and Germany. Francis also spends time teaching at universities. He has been a visiting professor at Harvard and Yale and holds a professorship at the Technical University of Munich.

Francis believes in using local African materials such as wood and clay to build and design modern structures. These materials have been used in building for centuries in Africa and are much better for the environment than synthetic materials.

"I USE DESIGN TO IMPROVE EDUCATION AND CREATE SUSTAINABLE BUILDINGS FOR MY PEOPLE."

Diébédo Francis

Iyinoluwa Aboyeji

Technology Innovator, Building Africa's Future
Lagos, Nigeria

Iyinoluwa has founded two of the fastest-growing technology companies in Africa and now spends his time working for the collective good of society.

Iyinoluwa was born in Nigeria and studied at Loyola Jesuit College, Abuja. He started his first company while he was at university in Canada.

After he graduated with a degree in legal studies, he moved back to Nigeria and founded his second company, Fora. Fora didn't go as planned but Iyinoluwa remained determined to build a successful company. He applied everything he had learnt from his previous businesses into his next company, Andela, which became Africa's largest technology resource, housing more than 1,000 developers and programmers.

In 2014, Iyinoluwa co-founded Flutterwave, a very successful online payments platform helping to connect Africa to the global economy.

Iyinoluwa understands that personal success does not protect one from the failures of society. When society fails to provide healthcare, security and jobs, even the most successful individuals can lose everything. It is for this reason that he founded Future Africa in 2019 to shape a better future for the continent.

Through Future Africa, Iyinoluwa provides entrepreneurs with money and coaching. He believes a prosperous future can be built by putting the collective interest of society above personal interests and is supporting businesses to do so. Iyinoluwa is also a World Economic Forum Young Global Leader.

"FROM A VERY EARLY AGE I KNEW MY WHOLE LIFE WOULD BE ABOUT HELPING TO BUILD THE FUTURE OF THE AFRICAN CONTINENT... EVERYTHING YOU SEE WAS BUILT BY SOMEONE WHO WAS NO SMARTER THAN YOU"

Iyinoluwa Aboyeji

Kelly Chibale

Scientist, Face of Chemistry
Mpika, Zambia

Kelly Chibale is a world-renowned scientist and professor of organic chemistry.

Kelly was born in Zambia and raised by his mother who was a market trader. He remembers growing up without electricity and running water in the Mpika district. In these conditions, Kelly saw education as a way out of poverty, and that made school both important and fun for him.

He studied chemistry at the University of Zambia before securing a scholarship to attend the University of Cambridge for his PhD as there were no opportunities for him to continue studying in Zambia.

Kelly had to work seven days a week for three years while at university just to keep up with other students who had come from better schools. Even during these years, Kelly loved learning, so it never really felt like work.

After his studies, he returned to Africa because he knew this was where he could really make an impact, inspire people and create jobs. Kelly was aware of the myth that Africa can't lead innovation or discover new drugs and medicines, so he focused his effort on proving this wrong.

Kelly now leads Africa's only drug discovery centre with its own drugs in Phase II clinical trials. His centre discovered a single-dose treatment for malaria in 2012. He is also in charge of 60 scientists working on pharmaceutical research at Cape Town University.

Kelly and his team have produced world-class innovations in chemistry and are funded by companies such as Novartis and Johnson & Johnson. He has been named by Fortune as one of the world's top 50 leaders and was elected a Fellow of the Royal Society of Chemistry.

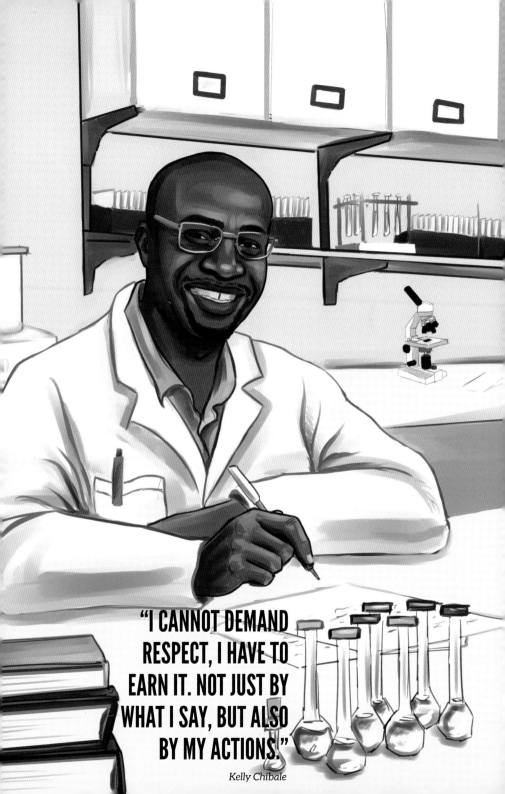

"I CANNOT DEMAND RESPECT, I HAVE TO EARN IT. NOT JUST BY WHAT I SAY, BUT ALSO BY MY ACTIONS."

Kelly Chibale

Kola Aina

Technology Investor and Entrepreneur
Kaduna, Nigeria

Kola has supported some of Africa's most promising technology startups by providing funding and mentorship to their founders.

Kola was born in Nigeria and went to school in Kaduna before moving to the USA to study electrical engineering at university. After completing his degree, Kola tried his hand at a few businesses before returning to Nigeria and setting up Emerging Platforms in 2010. Emerging Platforms takes problems and uses technology to solve them, such as helping schools and universities deliver their courses online.

Kola believes in the power of Africa's young population to drive change using technology. Following the success of Emerging Platforms, Kola decided to support other entrepreneurs and set up Ventures Platform to provide funding and mentorship to promising technology companies.

Through Ventures Platform, Kola has spent the last ten years helping companies that are solving some of the most serious problems in Africa. He has supported more than 30 companies across the healthcare, education, agriculture and financial industries, which have created thousands of jobs.Through Ventures Platform, Kola has spent the last ten years helping companies that are solving some of the most serious problems in Africa. He has supported more than 30 companies across the healthcare, education, agriculture and financial industries, which have created thousands of jobs.

While not every company succeeds, Kola views every investment as a learning opportunity. One of the companies he supported, Paystack, has gone on to become the highest-valued technology startup in Africa. Kola was selected for the prestigious Tutu Leadership Fellowship for 2020 and is a member of several Nigerian presidential advisory groups.

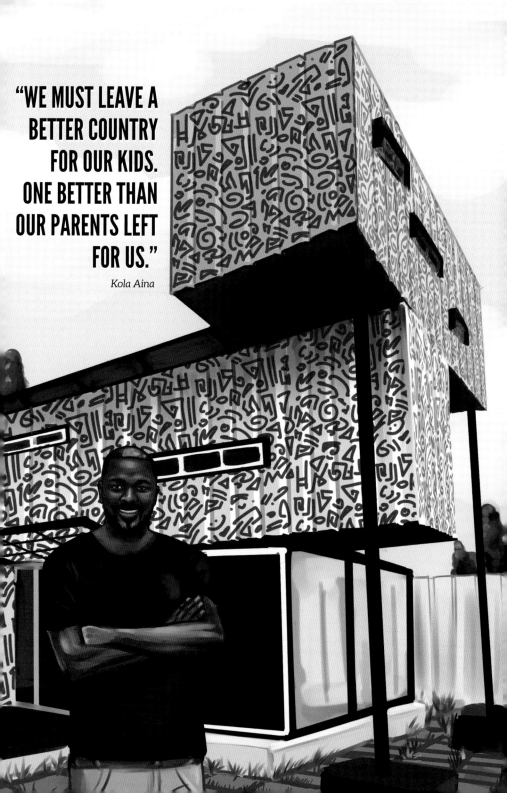

"WE MUST LEAVE A BETTER COUNTRY FOR OUR KIDS. ONE BETTER THAN OUR PARENTS LEFT FOR US."

Kola Aina

Oluyinka Olutoye

Doctor, Surgeon, Professor
Ondo , Nigeria

Dr Olutoye is known for healing babies and children through surgery.

Oluyinka remembers being a child growing up in Nigeria playing doctor and nurse games with his friends. Whenever a doctor came to visit his sick family members at home, Oluyinka would follow the doctor around to watch and learn everything. This was how he knew he wanted to be a doctor.

Oluyinka attended Kings College in Lagos, Nigeria, where he was one of the best students in his class. While at Kings College, he read a book written by the first person to perform a human heart transplant. This book sparked his interest to become a surgeon and he immediately began learning as much as he could about medicine and surgery.

After completing his degree at Kings College, Oluyinka attended Obafemi Awolowo University (OAU) in Nigeria to study medicine.

He graduated at the top of his class from OAU. Oluyinka then decided to move to North America, where he knew he would have access to the latest medical technology to become the best doctor he can be.

Oluyinka had a particular interest in embryos as a student. This interest, as well as a desire to identify and fix problems in the body, led him to focus his career in paediatric surgery.

In 2016, he led a team of 21 doctors to perform surgery on a baby before the baby was born. The doctors took the baby out of her mother's womb and placed her back into the womb safely after treating her.

In 2019, Oluyinka was appointed as Chief Surgeon at Nationwide Children's Hospital, one of the largest in the world.

"I'M LOOKING FORWARD TO OPPORTUNITIES THAT ALLOW ME TO CARE FOR EVEN MORE CHILDREN AND HAVE AN IMPACT. AS LONG AS WE TAKE IT ONE PATIENT AT A TIME... WE CAN HELP SOCIETY AT LARGE."

Kelly Chibale

Sossina M. Haile

Scientist
Addis Ababa, Ethiopia

Sossina is a Professor of Materials Science and Chemical Engineering and works to solve real problems in the world.

Sossina was born in Ethiopia and lived there until her father was arrested during a coup. After her father was released, her family relocated to the USA where she completed her education. She had loved science since she was a child and attended the Massachusetts Institute of Technology where she completed both her bachelor's degree and received a PhD in Materials Science and Engineering.

Sossina has gone on to become a leading world scientist. Sossina knows that global warming is a problem that should be taken seriously, and she has focused her work on finding solutions. As part of this, she produced the world's first solid acid fuel cells. These fuel cells can be used to produce electricity and power cars.

However, unlike petrol, which produces fumes that harm the environment, Sossina's fuel cells produce only water vapour when used. In addition to developing the fuel cell, she has also discovered new ways of using sunlight to produce energy.

Her work has gained her awards and recognition around the world, including the Chemical Pioneer Award and the Chow Foundation Humanitarian Award. In 2019, she was invited by Ethiopia as a keynote speaker to discuss the country's most pressing issues at the Ethiopia 2050 Conference.

"FOLLOW YOUR PASSION... DO NOT BE CONSTRAINED BY WHAT OTHERS THINK OF YOU!"

Sossina Haile

Leaders & Humanitarians

Clare Akamanzi

Development Professional, Lawyer
Ugandan born, From Rwanda

Clare Akamanzi is the public administrator at the centre of Rwanda's rebirth.

Clare was born in Uganda to refugee parents from Rwanda. She went to school in Uganda and graduated from Makerere University. She began her career at the World Trade Organization where she learnt about negotiating trade and investment deals between countries. Afterwards, she worked at the Rwandan embassy in London gaining experience in commerce.

But soon Clare decided to return to Rwanda where she believed she could make a difference. Her talent and work ethic attracted the most senior Rwandan government officials to her. After a few years of working in several government agencies and gaining a Master of Public Administration from Harvard University, she was appointed CEO of the Rwanda Development Board in 2017.

Under Clare and the Rwandan leadership, the country of Rwanda was reborn jinto a

place of beauty and one of the most popular destinations in Africa. Living conditions have improved and the economy has been rapidly industrialised.

Clare's vision is to transform Rwanda into a global hub for business. Rwandair has already become Africa's fastest growing airline and the World Bank has consistently ranked Rwanda as one of the easiest places to do business in Africa. The country is also rated as one of the least corrupt countries in Africa by Transparency International.

In 2018, Clare received an honorary doctorate degree from Concordia University for her contribution to improving the business environment and standards of living for Rwandans.

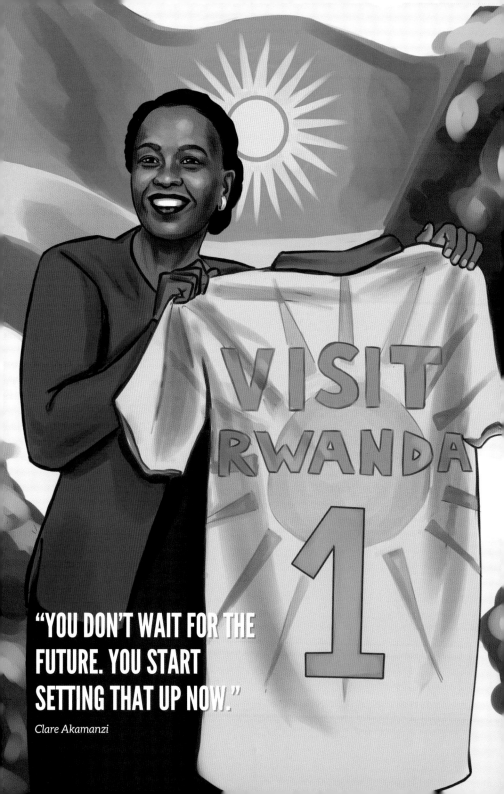

"YOU DON'T WAIT FOR THE FUTURE. YOU START SETTING THAT UP NOW."

Clare Akamanzi

Fatou Bensouda

Judge, Chief Prosecutor
Banjul, The Gambia

Fatou is the Chief Prosecutor at the International Criminal Court and works to make the world a safer place.

Fatou was born in The Gambia. Her father was a driver who had more than 12 other children. Fatou always had a good sense of fairness and justice. As a secondary school student, she saw that the most vulnerable people in her community were not receiving the protection that they needed from the government. She decided to do something about it and that was the beginning of her career in law and justice.

After she finished school in The Gambia, she left for university in Nigeria, where she graduated as a lawyer. Fatou then moved back home to work in her country.

She began her career as a state lawyer, and after a few years she was promoted and appointed as the country's Minister of Justice. At this time, Rwanda was recovering from a war a few years earlier, which had killed many people. Fatou began working to make sure that the people responsible for these deaths were punished. It was this experience that set her up to become the Chief Prosecutor of the International Criminal Court (ICC) in 2012.

The ICC was set up to bring justice to people who commit the most serious crimes one can imagine, usually during times of war. By punishing these people, the ICC discourages others from following in their footsteps.

Fatou has tried to make the world a safer and fairer place by investigating war crime charges against armies from numerous countries including Israel and the USA. In 2020, the USA responded by stopping Fatou from entering the country and blocking her from owning any property in the USA.

"I AM WORKING FOR THE VICTIMS OF AFRICA, THEY ARE AFRICAN LIKE ME. THAT'S WHERE I GET MY INSPIRATION AND PRIDE."

Fatou Bensouda

★ Tabitha Mpamira-Kaguri ★

Clinical Therapist, Girls Health Activist
Kigali, Rwanda

Tabitha has dedicated her life to stopping violence against girls and was the winner of the 2018 Global Citizen's Choice Award.

Tabitha grew up in Uganda as a Rwandan refugee. She later moved to the USA where she studied psychology at university and completed a Master of Arts in Clinical Psychology.

After completing her master's degree, she returned to Rwanda to help women and children who had been abused.

She started the EDJA Foundation after she met a few girls in Uganda who had survived violence by men. The EDJA Foundation's purpose is to fight against the abuse of children in every form.

The EDJA Foundation works to break the silence of abuse against girls and encourage more girls to speak up. Through community meetings and counselling, Tabitha encourages girls to come forward with their stories of abuse as a first step towards healing.

EDJA then provides free medical care and counselling to the girls. The final step EDJA takes is encouraging the police to punish the offenders.

Since Tabitha founded EDJA in 2015, she has spoken to over 3,000 people and helped hundreds of girls overcome the effects of abuse. Her ambition is to extend the work of EDJA across the entire continent. Her vision is for an Africa where every girl is protected from abuse.

69

"IT'S MY RESPONSIBILITY AND OBLIGATION TO BE PART OF SOCIAL CHANGE; TO BRING HEALING AND CREATE SPACE FOR LIGHT IN EVERY INDIVIDUAL I MEET."

Tabitha Mpamira-Kaguri

Wangari Maathai

Environmentalist, Nobel Prize Winner
Nyeri District, Kenya

Wangari Maathai was the first environmental scientist and African woman to win the Nobel Peace Prize.

Wangari was born in Nyeri, Kenya, the daughter of peasant farmers. As a child she spent a lot of time on the farm planting and harvesting crops with her parents. After school she went on to study biological sciences at university. She later became the first Eastern African woman to receive a PhD, with her doctorate from University of Nairobi.

Her first job was as a lecturer at the University of Nairobi, where she quickly realised that the challenge of preserving the environment must be addressed through government policies. She then resigned in order to campaign for a seat in parliament. After she was disqualified from running and could not get her job back, she founded the Green Belt Movement to help protect the environment and create jobs in local communities.

The movement has trained more than 30,000 women in forestry and planted more than 50 million trees.

Wangari led protests against the government in support of fair elections, women's rights and the preservation of natural parks. She later ran for parliament again and won with 98% of the vote. She was appointed as assistant minister in the Ministry of Environment and Natural Resources.

In 2004, she was awarded the Nobel Peace Prize for her contribution to democracy and global development. The Wangari Gardens was opened in Washington, D.C. in 2012 in honour of her legacy.

In Memory

1940 - 2011

"...IT DID NOT SEEM ODD TO ME TO WORK WITH MY HANDS, OFTEN WITH MY KNEES ON THE GROUND, ALONGSIDE RURAL WOMEN.. THE FUTURE OF OUR PLANET CONCERNS ALL OF US, AND ALL OF US SHOULD DO WHAT WE CAN TO PROTECT IT."

Wangari Maathai

Create Your Story

Profession: ....
Birth Country: ....

Your Portrait

Quote Sources

Page 1 "The Necessity of Aim" by Jordan Peterson, S2 E39"

Page 5 "...My grandmother sat me down and cleaned and braided my hair..."- Angelique Kidjo, during an interview with The Guardian in Paris, 2010

Page 12 "I'm an artist who wants to work in Africa..." - Ibrahim Mahama, during an interview with The Guardian in Manchester, 2019

Page 14 "As a brand, I want to reclaim the dignity and confidence..." - Laduma Ngxokolo, during an interview with Vogue, 2018

Page 23 "Caster Semenya row: 'Who are white people to question the makeup of an African girl? It is racism'" The Guardian, 2009

Page 26 "I have won many trophies..." - Didier Drogba, during an interview with The Telegraph, 2007

Page 29 "I was running on talent for a while..." - Siya Kolisi, Rugby World Magazine, 2018

Page 29 "South Africa Human Rights Commission report on South Africa released in 2018 highlights South Africa as the "most unequal country in the world"

Page 30 "When I walk out on the field..." - Siya Kolisi, during an interview with The Guardian, 2018

Page 32 "For people to be innovative…" – Bethlehem Alemu, during an interview with Reuters, 2016

Page 39 "I had no business training whatsoever…" Mo Ibrahim, on CNBC's The Brave Ones, 2019

Page 47 "I get up in the morning and I try to do my best…" Tidjane Thiam, Bloomberg, 2016

Page 54 "From a very early age…" Iyinoluwa Aboyeji, True Africa, 2016

Page 58 "I'm looking forward to opportunities…" Dr Oluyinka Olutoye, Virginia Commonwealth University News, 2017

Page 60 "Follow your passion…" Sossina Haile, Tadias Magazine interview, 2011

Page 66 "You don't wait for the future…" Clare Akamanzi, The Africa Report, 2018

Page 71 "Although I was a highly educated…" Wangari Maathai, Unbowed: My Autobiography, 2008